COMMUNICATING DURING A CRISIS

INFLUENCING OTHERS WHEN THE STAKES ARE HIGH

BY JOANNA DODD MASSEY, PH.D.

JDMA Publishing — New York

Communicating During a Crisis: Influencing Others When the Stakes Are High

Published by JDMA Publishing
45 Rockefeller Plaza, 20th Floor
New York, NY 10111
www.JDMAinc.com

ISBN-13: 978-0-578-67414-8
First Printing April 2020

This publication is designed to provide accurate and authoritative information in regard to the subject matter covered. It is sold with the understanding that the publisher is not engaged in rendering legal, accounting, or other professional service. If legal advice or other expert assistance is required, the services of a competent professional person should be sought. – From a Declaration of Principles Jointly Adopted by a Committee of the American Bar Association and a Committee of Publishers and Associations.

Some names and identifying details have been changed to protect the privacy of individuals. All brand names and product names used in this book are trademarks, registered trademarks or trade names of their respective holders.

Book Cover Design by Gian Colombo
Author Photos by Stephanie Simpson, Simpson Portraits
Edited by JDMA Publishing
JDMA Publishing is a subsidiary of J.D. Massey Associates™ Inc.

JOANNA DODD MASSEY, PHD

COMMUNICATING
DURING A CRISIS

Influencing Others
When The Stakes
Are High

TABLE OF CONTENTS

DEDICATION

This book is dedicated to my friend and
long-time business associate Jacquie Jordan,
who is a calm and reassuring voice during a crisis.

ACKNOWLEDGMENTS

I would like to thank my oldest friend in the world, John Franklin, for giving incredibly insightful notes on the book and also for writing the Foreword. I also want to thank Derek Fromson, who read the book and provided excellent feedback, as well as Sean Smith and Dr. Lydia Mallett for endorsing the book.

I have been running public relations departments at media companies since the late 1990s. In television, film and publishing, we are like a bug under a microscope. The audience has an intimate connection to our product, because they view it in their homes, bedrooms and, now that we have smartphones, everywhere they go. That means, when we do something wrong, we hear about it immediately. It is very hard to fly under the radar if you work in media.

I would like to acknowledge all of the executives with whom I have ever been through a crisis, but there have been so many, I could not name them all. There are some more memorable moments that stand out in my mind, so I would like to thank the colleagues who were in the trenches for those moments (this is in chronological order from the start of my career): Lisa Robinson, Rhonda Brauer and Jerry Epstein; Eric Schotz; Dawn Ostroff, Chris Ender, Gil Schwartz, Paul Hewitt, Cori Walworth, Rachel Seltzer, Carmen Davenporte McNeal, Rachel Clark and Larry Barron; Margaret Loesch, Dan Pimentel, Crystal Williams, Courtney Brown, Heather Smith, David Leavy and Julie Duffy; Peter Wilkes, Cristina Castañeda, Kevin Beggs and Ross Pollack.

Getting a doctorate in psychology changed my perspective on life and up leveled my understanding of humanity and how we respond in crises. I am indebted to the many teachers I had on the path to Ph.D., including Dr. Joy Turek; Dr. Victor Cohen; my MFT Trainee supervisor at Exodus Recovery, Richard Davis; Dr. Genie Palmer; Dr. Mark Gonnerman; Dr. Nicholas Kardaras; Dr. Judy Schavrien; and Reverend Keith Horwitz.

Like everyone, I have had innumerable personal trials and tribulations. I am blessed with family and friends who have ridden those waves. There are too many to mention, but I want to thank my mom Barbara Massey, my cousin Dan Massey, my godmother Lynn Ludlam, and many close friends whose names standout as having guided me through various crises of faith, including Rebecca Ascher-Walsh, Kristen Schlegel Cobbs, Amanda Cooper, Siddiqi Ray, Vanessa McGrady, Jennifer Grey, Camilla Outzen Rantsen, Jenny Davidson-Goldbronn, Rebecca Carpenter, Jude Roth, Marina Samaltanos, Jacquie Jordan and Erica Crystal Patterson.

FOREWORD

Search for a bit and you'll learn that the word "crisis" has medical origins. Hippocrates and Galen used it to refer to the turning point in a disease, when change means either recovery – or death. In ancient Greek the word relates to concepts like deciding, separating and judging. Put another way? Crisis is a Darwinian word, because it's about options and choices that threaten or guarantee survival.

So, not exactly an upbeat term. In fact, it's a pretty heavy one and that's exactly how most books, essays and plans about crises treat it: like a burden.

When Joanna told me she'd written this book and asked me to create a Forward for it, this baggage gave me pause. After all, the work was conceived and published during the COVID-19 pandemic – a frankly frightening time that fits both the historical and current definitions of a crisis to a "T."

Then I read the book.

And of course, like the author herself, it's authoritative but approachable – exactly the right mix of practical, truthful, funny and personal. In short, when it comes to the burden communicated by most other crisis experts, this book doesn't dwell on the weight. Instead, Joanna tells you how to carry it.

This was no surprise to me at least. It is rare in life that you get to say you've known someone since you were two years old, but Joanna and I can say just that. We met in pre-school when our parents lived in Boston. When we were four years old, both sets of parents moved back to New York City around the same time and remained friends. So, Joanna and I grew up together sharing Christmas dinners and summers in Fire Island. Coincidentally, she and I also both ended up working in communications managing corporate governance and crisis communications, though our paths diverged slightly – she went in-house for some of the biggest media companies in the world, and I went into consulting. That shared experience and perspective made it easy to recognize the value in what she's written here.

As the work itself explains, this is as much a psychology handbook as it is a business one, and one of its strengths is that it tells the truth about the many unspoken links between what's usually considered business and what's normally thought of as personal. Now, business and personal have always blurred. But today we've got five different generations in the workplace for the first time, at scale. Younger generations, not surprisingly, feel and talk differently than older ones about personal/business boundaries, or lack thereof. Many crises spring from exactly this reality.

Joanna's experience running communications divisions for major corporations, and her multiple degrees in psychology, help make sense of all this in a way that will be new to many, and useful to all.

That's a book for our time. Because if you and/or your businesses are facing a crisis – and right now, arguably all of us are – you don't need someone else telling you we're in a dumpster that's on fire. You need thoughtful, positive counsel on how to cope.

Look no further.

John Franklin III
Founder & Partner, Sinter

INTRODUCTION | I KNOW I'M RIGHT, SO WHY WON'T THEY LISTEN?!

"I have a 15 and a 14 year old and the more I tell them not to do something, the more they do it!"[1]

That was United States Surgeon General Dr. Jerome Adams, who had gone on *Good Morning America* (GMA) on March 19, 2020 to plead with America's youth to practice social distancing (maintaining physical distance from others in order to stop the spread of a contagious disease).

At the time, the world was in the throes of a pandemic. COVID-19, which stands for coronavirus disease 2019 and was also popularly referred to as coronavirus, had quickly made its way to every continent around the globe and it was spreading rapidly throughout the United States. Subsequently, images were emerging of young people widely disregarding health warnings to stay indoors and keep a safe distance from others.

The Surgeon General continued, "We need to get our social media influencers out there and helping folks understand that, look, this is serious. This is absolutely serious. People are dying."[2]

During the interview with three of GMA's anchors, the Surgeon General also told GMA's audience, "The two best things you can do to protect yourself and your community are good hygiene—hand washing—and social distancing. Stay off the beaches."

GMA anchor Robin Roberts then asked Dr. Adams, "Can you help people understand that? Because, I know we keep hearing that about don't touch your face and washing your hands. Can you just emphasize that it may seem small, but they have a significant impact on what's happening?"

And there is was. Roberts had asked the million-dollar question. Essentially, what she was saying was to Dr. Adams was: I know you're right, so why aren't they listening?

#FlattentheCurve: Why Some Millennials and Gen Zers Ignored the Coronavirus Crisis

The worldwide crisis created by a new strain of coronavirus disease called COVID-19 seemingly began in late 2019. It first ravaged China, then South Korea, Italy and Iran. As it spread like wildfire around the globe, the World Health Organization declared COVID-19 a pandemic on March 11, 2020.[3]

The United States seemed largely unaffected with a few sporadic cases until March 2020. The country went from 24 people testing positive for COVID-19 and one death on February 29, 2020[4] to 140,904[5] cases and 2,454 deaths[6] a month later on March 29, 2020. That is a massive increase and those numbers only account for those who were tested at the time.

In order to halt the spread of COVID-19, schools, restaurants, entertainment venues and businesses around the United States closed rapidly. Vibrant cities became ghost towns as health officials warned everyone to stay inside. The stock market plummeted and, on March 9, 2020, it experienced its worst single-day drop since the Great Recession in 2008.[7] Many states ordered residents to stay at home, except to get food, medical attention and other essential services. #FlattentheCurve trended on social media, and the United States—along with the entire world—was thrown into a health crisis and subsequent economic downturn the likes of which it had not seen in several generations.

There have been other pandemics in modern times. Some less lethal than others, but all serious, including a flu pandemic in 1968 that killed 1 million people, one from 1956-1958 with 2 million fatalities, and one in 1918, which killed an estimated 20-50 million people.[8] While this was not the first time the world had experienced a pandemic, it was the first for many younger people, who either panicked or totally disregarded warnings to practice the new concepts of social distancing, self-isolating and self-quarantining.

Photos and videos of college kids on spring break and young adults in crowded bars went viral on social media as older generations blamed and shamed the younger ones for being selfish and entitled. Health officials, government authorities and opinion news commentators from Fox News and CNN admonished Millennials (born 1981-1996) and Generation Z (born 1997-2012)[9] for not practicing social distancing.[†]

It is at this point that an experienced practitioner—or a thoughtful person—might realize the essential difficulty in communicating during a crisis. Blame is easy, criticisms rapid, while influence and desired outcomes are hard.

Instead of jumping to conclusions and blaming and shaming, let us first ask, "Why?"

[†] There is disagreement in social sciences research about the birth years of all of the generations, but especially Generation Z. The years I use here are Pew Research numbers. I wrote another book called *Culture Shock: Surviving Five Generations in One Workplace*, in which I quote a different generational expert and explain that he thinks Gen Z ends in 2010. These birth years are yet to be reckoned, so I wanted to make note of it given the competing birth-year information in my own books!

Why were these young adults ignoring the very serious warnings that they needed to #FlattentheCurve through social distancing and self-isolation? Were they in fact ignoring them, or was something else causing the issue?

I have a Ph.D. in psychology, an MBA and more than 25 years as a communications executive (when I am being honest, it is actually 30 years). I spent my career in the media industry promoting to and working with 18-to-34-year-olds. Currently, I work as a consultant and corporate speaker advising clients on communicating with their Millennial and Gen Z consumers, employees and investors.

As an expert in communicating with young adults, and as someone who looks at everything in business through a psychological lens, I will give you two reasons why America's youth apparently ignored the social distancing directive.

1. At the start of the COVID-19 outbreak, all of the messaging was about the virus being lethal for people over 60 years old and for those with compromised immune systems. America's youth were told for weeks that this particular strain of coronavirus was only deadly for older people or those with certain pre-existing conditions.

2. Health officials, the government, and even the media were not reaching younger Millennials and Gen Z. In 2020, there were three primary ways to reach young adults in the United States— and the initial public health messaging failed to leverage any of them:
   - Use video
   - Have a peer convey the message
   - Post it on TikTok, Snapchat, Instagram and YouTube

Up until mid-March, officials only used traditional media to communicate with Americans. This meant they were reaching only about 50 percent of the population.

Communicating is about being targeted with your message, method and medium. This is something that every public relations (PR) and marketing person knows, but it may not be widely understood outside of those specialties. So, as I tell my graduate students at Columbia University, where I teach corporate communications: Many of the standard ways that organizations use to inform their consumers during a crisis no longer work.

The resulting situation during the COVID-19 pandemic—during which many young people were flouting critical medical advice—served as a much-needed wake-up call to the news media, government officials and health authorities. It became clear they have to meet America's youth where they are at and speak to them in a language they can relate to, if they want to influence them.

By the time Dr. Adams went on GMA to address the issue of young people scoffing at orders to self-isolate, regulators were finally catching on to the problem. That is presumably why Dr. Adams made sure to name-check specific social media influencers, including Kylie Jenner. He called on them to use their platforms to convey the seriousness of the pandemic and the need for social distancing.[10]

Jenner responded quickly. Within hours, she posted a message to her 166 million followers on Instagram that urged them to stay inside and told them what she had been doing to occupy herself during self-isolation.[11]

At the same time, other celebrities and organizations realized the message was not reaching young people. Social media campaigns started to appear on Instagram, TikTok and the like. Kevin Bacon created a "six degrees" social media game to try to encourage people to self-isolate.[12] The World Health Organization (WHO) launched a livestreaming concert series called "Together at Home" with huge musical acts like John Legend, Coldplay and others to encourage people to stay home.[13]

Dr. Anthony Fauci, who oversees the National Institute of Allergy and Infectious Diseases (NIAID) and is a member of U.S. President Donald Trump's White House Coronavirus Task Force, also started to connect with younger generations. In March 2020, he appeared on Trevor Noah's *Daily Social Distancing Show* and an Instagram Live talk with basketball phenom Stephen Curry of the Golden State Warriors.

The idea that influence is not the same as communications is true for people, businesses and governments. It also crosses generations, which is why I wrote this book.

This is a communications book with a self-help bent, because in order for you to understand how to be an effective communicator, you also have to know what people go through emotionally during a crisis. So, the first three chapters of this book are dedicated to discussing what constitutes a crisis and how human beings respond emotionally and physiologically during those times.

Do not let that last sentence fool you. This is not a dry textbook analysis of crisis communications. My writing style is colloquial and personal. Why? Because the most influential communicators personalize their message so that it resonates for people.

When you are done with this book, you will understand how human beings react to crises; you will have a list of crisis communications practices used by the pros; and you will have a simple (but not easy) three-step process for influencing people when the stakes are high.

One more note before moving into the chapter content. The advice that I am offering in this book played out in a major way in 2020 during the coronavirus pandemic. Therefore, what I say in the book is not just abstract academic thinking or my experience of 30 years, it is the intersection of communications and human behavior. Done right, it can literally save lives and, done wrong, it can kill people and destroy businesses.

CHAPTER 1 | WHAT CONSTITUTES A CRISIS?

I am going to begin at the beginning—by examining what a crisis is, because there are as many definitions of what constitutes a crisis as there are human beings on the planet. Some people think of a crisis as a very big event in their life. Yet, many of us know individuals who seem to constantly be in a state of crisis. Whether the problem occurs in your personal or professional life, an earth-shattering event to one person can be a big nothing burger to someone else.

The reality is that crises are about how we internalize what is happening to us. Our mental and emotional reaction then dictates how we manage the situation in our external world.

Starting with the biggest and most obvious scenario, crises can be worldwide and globally devastating. So, pandemics, such as COVID-19 and the Spanish Flu in 1918; economic downturns, such as the Great Recession in 2008 and the Great Depression from 1929-1939; and acts of aggression, such as the September 11 attack on the United States or World War II, during which 85 million people were killed.

Of course, crises can happen to businesses, and they come in all shapes and sizes. They include:

- Environmental—The Exxon Valdez and Deepwater Horizon oil spills are examples.
- Financial losses and employee layoffs—This happens in Hollywood whenever one of the unions strike. Movies and TV series cannot get made without actors, so companies shut down production, there are no jobs for industry workers, and employees at big studios and television networks get laid off. In 2007, a Writers

Guild Strike lasted nearly 100 days and led to big layoffs at the studios.[14]

- Product boycotts—In the social media age, product boycotts happen regularly. Offended viewers boycotted the NFL during the 2017 season when many football players would "take a knee" during the playing of the National Anthem to protest police violence in African American communities and to support freedom of speech. On the other side of the political spectrum, consumers boycotted Chick-fil-A after it was revealed that corporate profits were used to donate to anti-LGBTQ organizations.

- Consumer deaths—You may know about Johnson & Johnson's famous Tylenol tampering case in the 1980s or the Jack in the Box E. coli outbreak in the early 1990s. These situations caused significant economic impact to the companies, both of which recovered thanks to their top-notch crisis responses.

- Accidental deaths or workplace violence—There are some industries where workplace accidents happen more frequently, including manufacturing, shipping, construction, installation and emergency services.[15] Intentional violence, however, is more commonplace than it once was. Starting in the 1990s, a slew of shootings by United States postal workers coined the term "going postal," which became a catch-all phrase for workplace violence.

Finally, crises happen in our personal lives. Certainly, a worldwide pandemic or a crisis at the organization where we work can kick off a personal problem, but so can a variety of issues that are unique to our individual circumstances, including the death of a loved one, loss of a job, a frightening medical diagnosis, alcohol or drug abuse, or financial stress.

Crises Don't Just Happen in Midlife

Now that we have an overview of the different types of crises, let us examine what exactly a crisis is.

I believe in looking up words in the dictionary, because I think I have a good command of the English language, but I sometimes find that I have twisted the meanings of certain words over a lifetime of using them.

"Perfect" is one of those words. I used it against myself for years, because I thought there was a perfect ideal that I had not achieved. I thought there was a perfect way for me to behave, a perfect way for me to think, a perfect way for me to look, a perfect way for me to be, and a perfect life for me to have.

I had made up a story in my head—*The Rules of Life According to Joanna*—and then used it as a means by which to judge myself and my life. Unfortunately, I always fell short.

The reason I could not live up to it was because the ideal had been developed by a five-year-old, who thought the perfect woman knows everything at her job and never makes any mistakes at work. She gets along with everyone and no one ever gets mad at her. She is hugely successful in business and she gets there by being the perfect worker, with the perfect husband, the perfect house, a dog and 2.3 kids[16] (this was a much-mocked statistic from the 1970s about the average number of kids in an American household).

My idea of perfection was a combination of the American Dream coupled with a child's understanding of what it means to be a grownup. After a few decades of using this concept of perfection to make myself feel badly about who I was, what I said, and what I did, I finally looked up the word perfect in the dictionary.

It means "without fault or defect."[17]

At first glance, that definition is not encouraging. Most people who are perfectionists are desperately trying to compensate for perceived faults and defects. Then I really started to think about it, and I had an epiphany.

At my very core, what am I? I am a human being.

I can assign a lot of other identities to myself as a human being, such as female, New Yorker, daughter, executive, ex-wife, etc. But the bottom line is that I am none of those things without first being a human being.

What does it take to be a perfect human being? It turns out that it does not take any effort at all. It is what I actually am. If I went to a doctor right now, no matter what character flaws I have, the doctor would not say to me, "I'm sorry. You have a defect so big that I have to declare you part tiger and part human."

This realization was very liberating for me. No matter what we do as human beings, no matter what we say and no matter what we think, it is all perfectly human. Of course, depending on the people in your life and how you feel about them, that revelation can be a little more difficult to swallow.

If that is the case, I recommend looking into the powerful feature-length documentary *The Prison Within*.[18] It is about a restorative justice program at San Quentin for violent offenders. It is a perception-changing movie. Directed and produced by women and independently made, it was winning awards on the film festival circuit when the COVID-19 pandemic struck. It quickly found a distributor and was slated to be available on-demand in late 2020.

Let us get back to how this all ties into our discussion about communicating during a crisis. In our minds, each of us has written a book called, *The Rules of Life According to Me*, which we walk around with throughout our lives. We all have an idea about how we think life should be.

When life differs dramatically from what we consider "normal"… well, that becomes a crisis.

There are a few definitions under the word "Crisis" in the dictionary. They include (1) an unstable time and period of change and (2) "an emotionally significant event or radical change of status in a person's life."[19]

Depending on your personality and disposition, there are a lot of things that could be perceived as significant events or unstable times that cause a period of change. Change is constant and with the hyper-frenetic pace of technology, communications and activity, disruptive events happen constantly. It would be completely understandable if people across the world frequently felt like they were in some sort of crisis.

You may recall that Benjamin Franklin famously said death and taxes are the only two things that are certain in life. I am going to parse that further. Death and taxes have something in common—they create a change in your life. So, I think there is only one certainty in life, and that is change!

True as that might be, it is equally correct to note that, as human beings, we are biologically hardwired to resist change. This makes handling crises—and the often dramatic changes that come with them—challenging for us. It also makes communicating with others during crises doubly hard. That is why the next part of this book talks about our neurological responses to stress.

Given my background, my job is to take complex concepts and make them easily digestible. So, what comes next will not be in any standard textbook about neuroscience. I have read those books, so you do not have to do it. Instead, what you are about to read is the way I describe brain processes to friends over the dinner table.

So, grab a glass of wine and enjoy the read. For the next two chapters, we will cover neuroplasticity and human emotional responses. Because, in my experience, effective communications start with something that we all share: the body's unconscious responses to stress. If you do not start by understanding what triggers people's anxieties, you cannot influence them effectively.

CHAPTER 2 | THE FEAR FACTOR

Human beings mark time with change. We determine the time of day by the changing positions of the sun and the moon in the sky. We determine the time of year by the change in weather and foliage on the trees. We determine our age by all of the changes we experience from cradle to grave.

When people are in the midst of a crisis, they frequently say things like, "Did that only happen two days ago? It seems like a month went by!" Or, "Has it only been a week? It felt like a year!"

During a crisis, we have the feeling that time has sped up because a crisis brings a lot of change and we equate change with time lapse. The amount of change we experience during a crisis increases exponentially from what we are accustomed to in our day-to-day lives, so it feels like more time is passing than actually is.

Yet, as common as it is for us to experience this kind of time expansion, it is even more common for human beings to reject the change that accelerated time represents. It does not matter that change is inevitable; most people hate it!

A good illustration of this aversion can be found in the success of a popular 1990s business book called *Who Moved My Cheese?*[20] It is a motivational story about dealing with change at work and in life. If you read a summary of the plot, it sounds like a children's book—four characters search for cheese in a maze. Yet, as a business parable, it has few peers—28 million copies sold to date. Why? The way it characterizes resistance to change is frank, on point and relatable.

This brings me to my first key point—people under stress are naturally inclined to fight against change and dig into their existing beliefs and practices. So, let us explore where the resistance to change starts.

There is a part of our brain called the amygdala, which starts getting programmed *in utero.* It stores the emotional responses to everything that happens in our lives. It is a complex computer program with unlimited capacity. The amygdala is responsible for our unconscious and immediate responses to danger, so it is programmed to remember negative experiences more strongly than positive ones.

Since the amygdala starts getting programmed when we are kids, its reactions to life are based on all of our experiences growing up. It develops a story that is unique to each of us about what we like and do not like, what is right and what is wrong, how things should be and how they should not be.

Not surprisingly, we are literally rooted in this story. After all, it is our beliefs, which are hard coded into our brains. The amygdala has helped us write that internal book I mentioned earlier—*The Rules of Life According to Me.*

You may have heard of unconscious bias. The Oxford Reference definition is "Any distortion of experience by an observer or reporter of which they are not themselves aware. This includes the processes of unintentional selectivity and transformation involved in perception, recall, representation, and interpretation..."[21]

The amygdala sets our baseline—our unconscious but very powerful comfort zone—against which we map everyday events. Moreover, this unconscious baseline is inherently more negative, because it was built to keep us safe from threats.

How does it do that? It takes a lot of the slower, conscious thinking out of the equation, in order to allow us to simply react. So that amygdala-driven reaction—that comfort zone—is change averse. I am going to go into more detail about that in the next section.

Lions and Tigers and Bears, Oh My!

Dorothy, Tin Man and the Scarecrow turned their fears into a song, as they skipped through the dark forest chanting, "Lions and tigers and bears, oh my!"[22] This could be the amygdala's theme song.

Before the song, however, the characters expressed hesitation, doubt and fear. The scene starts with the three stopping in fear as they debate whether or not it is safe to go into the unknown forest on their journey to meet the Wizard of Oz. A perfect enactment of what the amygdala does in a split second.

Let us examine why communications get more difficult during crises, because it is not your imagination. As human beings, it is harder for us to process information logically and there is a biological reason for it.

The front part of our brain is called the prefrontal cortex and it controls a system commonly known as executive functioning. Not surprisingly, it got its nickname because it is responsible for the part of the brain that handles actions that we equate with being an executive—problem solving, rational decision making and self-control. All good and very helpful tools that could really help during a crisis.

There is just one problem. When we hit a certain level of maximal stress, the prefrontal cortex—the "executive"—is no longer in charge. It is the amygdala that is responsible for calming down the system. The amygdala takes its job very seriously and it has total authority. It is a bit of a dictator in that way.

First, it shuts down the prefrontal cortex so that there are not any contradictory commands during the crisis.

After all, you would not want the amygdala telling you to run, while the prefrontal cortex is telling you to be rational and think about it for a second. Obviously, you cannot have two generals issuing contradictory orders.

I am going to pause here, because I want to make sure what I just said is clear: When we get stressed, the amygdala shuts down the part of the brain responsible for rational thinking and self-control.

Second, the amygdala searches the memory banks for historical information about what helps calm down the body. This response is as unique as every individual on the planet. The answer to what calms down your system has to do with every experience you have had in your life and how the amygdala processed it in the past, because the amygdala learns from past experiences.

Someone who struggles with alcoholism or compulsive eating will, thanks to the amygdala, turn to alcohol or food in periods of high stress, unless they have trained their brain on other ways to de-stress. Someone who lashes out in anger when they are stressed will become enraged. Someone who finds comfort in binge watching TV will turn to that habit, as opposed to face what needs to be done to cope with the problem.

These responses are popularly known as fight, flight or freeze. Why? Because everything we do in response to stress can be boiled down to one of those three overarching themes.

The good news is that the brain can be retrained, although it is impossible to shut off the amygdala's function entirely—nor would we want to. The amygdala is one of the most ancient parts of our brain and it was developed in order to help us in life-or-death situations, such as, "There is a tiger behind that tree."

In a life-or-death situation, we do not have time to think, "Hey, I think I just heard a growl. I bet that is a tiger. I better run. Ok, now I am running."

You most certainly do not want the prefrontal cortex trying to rationalize with you in that moment: "Hey, are you sure that's a tiger? What if it isn't? You're sure going to look stupid to your cavemen buddies if you start running now and it isn't a tiger."

If our brains had to take the time to go through that thought process, the tiger would be happily eating us for dinner before we had finished rationally debating what to do next. The amygdala handles all of that for us automatically and unconsciously. In fact, thanks to the amygdala, we do not need to consciously hear the growl. We can often start running or jump out of the way without fully realizing why. That is the amygdala at work, and it is helpful.

Today, there are rarely tigers behind the trees, but the amygdala does not know that, so it can treat being late to work like a life-or-death situation. If you have ever gotten caught in traffic trying to get to an important meeting and started screaming like a lunatic at the other drivers—who are also stuck in cars that are not moving—you can thank your amygdala for that reaction.

Retrain Your Brain

Knowing how the amygdala functions and what triggers fight, flight or freeze can help us counteract it. You can, with time and effort, retrain your brain to stay calm in situations that might otherwise result in a high-stress reaction.

The brain has the ability to continually change throughout our lives thanks to neuroplasticity. The word neuroplasticity is a mashup word derived from neurons and plasticity.

The neurons, which are nerve cells in your brain, wire together to make connections needed for everyday functioning. The neurons are constantly making new connections to help the brain learn and store information.

Plasticity means that the nerve cells are easily shaped or molded.

These two functions together enable us to retrain our brains and get rid of some of the old programming that dictates our automatic responses, which were formed in childhood. Scientists have a saying for remembering this concept:

The neurons that fire together, wire together.

It means that by constantly feeding the brain new inputs related to a calm, positive feeling, your brain can rewire and so reprogram.

Switching back to communications for a moment, what all this means is that every day working life presents most people with enough stress to trigger unconscious fight, flight or freeze reactions. While we cannot know and address all of the individual manifestations of these reactions—who needs a donut vs. a couch and a TV—we can bear in mind the fact that these very physical triggers exist. This means that we should stop thinking about successful communications as simply "rationally conveyed and rationally understood information." The next chapter looks at tools for dealing with people under stress.

For now, bear in mind that we can take steps to work on our own reactions to stress. One popular method to retrain your brain is to develop a mantra that you repeat over and over while sitting calmly. For example, if your company is hiring a lot of younger employees who are making changes that your boss loves, but you are resistant to, a good mantra is, "Let go and let the change happen." If you are religious, you can alter that to the popular spiritual saying, "Let go and let God."

Call it a jingle if that term works better for you than the word mantra. Either way, it helps if the phrase is memorable. All the better if the wording has alliteration or rhymes.

I used to resist change until it dawned on me that life would be less stressful if I could retrain my brain to enjoy the twists and turns life takes. I have a few mantras that I use. One of them is the following:

Lighten the F up! Things always work out.

I say it to myself a few times a day. When I get tense, "lighten the F up" reminds me that the ups and downs are normal. It also makes me laugh, because I remember that 90 percent of the things that I worry about never happen.

Admittedly, it is not always possible in that moment for me to let go of whatever is making me tense. However, the thought reminds me of the bigger picture—the one beyond that single moment—and it gives my amygdala a new baseline.

The mantra and deep breaths I take when I say it have become such an automatic part of my mind's process that as soon as I feel stress, the thought to "lighten up" pops into my thinking, because I have trained the unconscious part of my brain. Instead of lashing out at someone or eating an entire chocolate cake, the action that my amygdala takes to calm me down is twofold: first, it reminds me of my mantra and, second, it instructs my body to take a nice deep breath.

It is a simple practice that requires regular repetition. One thing I do is set the "Reminders" app on my phone to go off every few hours with a mantra. This helps me stay on task with my thinking throughout the day, which can get crazy busy with emails, calls, meetings and other activity.

I work with business executives coaching them on myriad issues from getting better results from their teams to yielding more influence in a meeting or presentation. If you have the capacity for personal insight and can be honest with yourself, you can work through old belief systems that are holding you back. But that is a topic for another book!

In *this* book, you are likely starting to see why I said in the Introduction that it would combine business communications tools and self-help guidelines. So, now that we have a better understanding of the brain function that kicks in during stressful periods, we are next going to explore how this manifests in human emotions and behaviors. As I said earlier, in order to effectively communicate with people during a crisis, it really helps to grasp what they are experiencing internally.

CHAPTER 3 | EMOTIONAL & BEHAVIORAL REACTIONS TO FEAR

A t a certain point in life, we are taught to toughen up. In America, we say things like, "Boys don't cry," while women are told, "Put on your big girl pants and deal with it." The British have made an art of giving stoic reactions in the face of adversity. Their popular saying, "Keep a stiff upper lip," is worn like a badge of honor.

Regardless, we are human beings and these bodies come with emotions. We cannot avoid them and we cannot stop them; they come no matter what we do. We can pretend our emotions are not happening. We can try to stuff them down. We can numb them out with drugs, alcohol, food, gambling or sex. No matter how each of us handles our own emotions, we cannot stop the physiological response.

Here is a nonnegotiable, biological truth: what we think, we feel.

If we think something depressing, we may feel a heavy weight in our chest or a tightness in our stomach. If we are excited, our skin may tingle, we may feel a surge of energy and our body may feel lighter. If we are scared, our breathing can become labored and short, while our pulse quickens and our glands sweat. These are unavoidable physiological responses to the thoughts we are having in our minds.

It is important to know these things when you are trying to communicate with and influence people during a crisis. Whether you are running a company, a country or a family, what follows are some of the typical behavioral and emotional reactions that happen during a crisis.

SCARFing: It Is Not A Fashion Statement

The human brain has one very important job—survival. The brain asks all day long, "Is it safe?"

Throughout the day, the brain unconsciously assesses the situations it is in: Is this person safe? Is this conversation safe? Is this work environment safe? Is this train ride safe? Is this dog safe? Is this car safe? Is this rollercoaster ride safe?

The mind may use a different word than "safe," but if you dig deep, and honestly explore your motives for every judgement you make all day long (and who has time for that), you can see that the root of your motive is the question, "Is it safe?"

If the answer is yes, it is safe, then the brain functions as normal and you have no idea it has made that assessment. If the answer is no, it is not safe, then the amygdala kicks in and that is when knowing about SCARF is very helpful!

SCARF is rooted in neuroscience and it is a theory about how to influence people.[23] It was developed by Dr. David Rock, who runs the Neuroscience Leadership Institute, which brings a scientific approach to the softer skills of effective management and leadership.

Dr. Rock posits that employees who feel threatened at work will have predictable responses, because feeling threatened will trigger the amygdala's fight, flight or freeze response. He organized his theory into the acronym SCARF. It is based on risk and reward behaviors and, since that sounds like psychobabble, let me delve into that concept further. SCARF stands for the following:

Status—This is about your rank or position with others (work, family, friends, community).

Certainty—The brain loves certainty, so this involves familiarity and knowing where you stand—the ability to predict what is coming (it is a problem when your mind's crystal ball is cloudy and not clear).

Autonomy—This is about freedom. What freedom do you have to make decisions at home and at work?

Relatedness—This involves relating to others. Ask yourself: How well do I get along with others in my personal and professional life? Am I experiencing conflicts with my boss or coworkers? This also applies to family and friends.

Fairness—This concerns your idea of justice. Am I being treated fairly or are others getting better treatment than me?

Rock's theory hypothesizes that if any of these areas are threatened, i.e., any of them do not pass the brain's safety test, then that person will be stressed. A few examples:

- Your business sector is being disrupted by a new technology that is upsetting your old way of operating (think: what Netflix has done to traditional television viewing). As a result, your company is experiencing huge financial losses. The CEO and management team have devised a plan to turn it around by investing in a new technology to compete with the disruptive changes, but it will be at least another 18 months before the company is making a profit again. With the massive changes happening at the company, every employee feels threatened at all five levels—status, certainty, autonomy, relatedness and fairness.

- During a massive turnaround in operations, your company brings in managers who are more knowledgeable about implementing the new technology. You get a new boss and that person does not approve of how you do your job. Your status, certainty and autonomy are threatened.

- Your wife comes home cranky from work every night because she has a new boss who is changing everything and she is worried that she will get fired. She takes it out on you, so the two of you fight constantly for months. Your relatedness and fairness are threatened.
- Your mom and dad are fighting a lot over work stuff and, on top of that, you are being bullied at school. Your certainty, relatedness and fairness are threatened.

In all of these examples, the individuals are SCARFing, so their amygdala will frequently be in the driver's seat. During stress, our decision making may be emotional, as opposed to rational.

It is worth repeating here that the amygdala is an unconscious operator. That means our emotional response may seem perfectly rational to us when we are under stress, but others will look at us like we have five heads when we tell them our plan.

There are different ways to help someone who is experiencing one of these five problems. For example, if someone feels their **status** is threatened, you can praise them publicly, which will help meet their need to feel appreciated and respected for what they do.

If **certainty** is in question, try to assure the person. If that is not possible (as is the case with the fictitious company in massive disruption), try to reframe the negative as a positive. After all, change brings opportunity. Additionally, if you can give an individual a choice about what happens next, it is helpful. People have a sense of being in control when they have options to choose from—even if none of the choices are ideal.

If their **autonomy** is being taken away, again giving someone options is helpful. They have a sense that they get to choose an outcome for themselves.

If they do not seem to be **relating** well with others, make small talk with them and go out of your way to include them in conversations, meetings or projects.

When the issue is **fairness**, people need to feel like they are being heard. It is important that their perspective is understood and considered. Only then, can it be discussed rationally. Since it is often the case that the individual will continue to view the outcome as unfair, work with that person to find opportunities for him or her. Where are the silver linings in the situation?

At this point, you may be thinking to yourself that SCARF seems to work great when one-on-one but wondering if it can work on a companywide level. The answer is yes.

Companies comprise people. In aggregate, they are huge behemoths, but in reality, they are individual squads working alongside each other to form an army that carries out the mission of running the company. When people are SCARFing, it is helpful to be more mindful about how you interact with your employees in order to get the outcomes you would like. This is true when you are dealing with one family member, 10,000 employees, or 10 million citizens. Following is an example of how that can work.

Whether you are talking to an individual or a group, if you know their **certainty** is being jeopardized, give them options. Using our fictitious company that is shifting its business model, management could offer early retirement plans or buyouts to workers as a way to trim payroll costs and to eliminate employees whose skills will not transfer to the new technology being introduced. This gives the employees the option of staying or taking the buyout. They will feel more in control, because they have a choice in their fate. It also makes the transition period smoother, because the employees who choose to stay want to be there and help the organization. Giving them a choice positively impacts their **status, relatedness** and **fairness**.

Keep in mind that the primary survival trigger for human beings is the concept of safety. But we do not all share a universal definition of what safety is because it means different things to different people. Safety can come from being surrounded by a strong family unit. Safety can be found in a job that allows you to have a lifestyle that suits you. Some people equate owning a home with safety.

Regardless of what makes you feel safe, one thing is certain, if you do not feel safe, fear kicks in and stress arises. When fear strikes, it is the amygdala's job to step in and take over functioning.

The 5 Stages of Grief

Besides the neuroscientific response we experience in a crisis, there are also significant emotional responses. Certainly, the two are related, but I make the distinction here because fight, flight and freeze are very specific behaviors that can include a nearly infinite number of emotional responses that accompany them.

Elisabeth Kübler-Ross was a noted psychiatrist who developed a famous theory known as the five stages of grief. She identified the stages as: denial, anger, bargaining, depression and acceptance.[24]

Kübler-Ross' work focused on death and the shock that comes with it, but her theory has been applied to innumerable situations where we experience any significant loss negatively. Getting fired from a job, breaking up with a significant other, and being forced into self-isolation by an invisible virus praying on humanity are all situations that could create a sense of loss that can emotionally feel like we have experienced a death.

It is common for people who are experiencing a major life change to go through the Kübler-Ross stages. Let us say that a company experiences massive layoffs and you lose your job unexpectedly, along with 20 percent of your colleagues. Initially, there is the shock. That is the precursor to the emotional rollercoaster you will then experience, which are the five stages of grief.

First comes denial: "Losing my job is not a problem. I will get another one quickly. They may even hire me back in a few weeks when they realize they laid off too many people and they need me, so this could be like an unexpected vacation."

After that is anger: "How dare they fire me! The people running the company are all idiots. It is no surprise that they mismanaged it into this mess. I am going to go on social media and let everyone know exactly what I think about that company and their bad business practices!"

Next stage is bargaining. In this stage, you are usually negotiating with yourself or your concept of something bigger than yourself. "Ok, let's make a deal. I will collect unemployment and spend the next few months looking for a job as opposed to lying on the couch, and you will bring me a bigger and better job than the one I had. Sound good to you?!"

Then comes depression. There is a point when sadness kicks in and, in some cases, it can feel overwhelming. The loss of the job, your work family, colleagues, the daily schedule that structured your life and the lack of income become heavy and scary. "I don't know when this unsure time will end. When will things get back to normal?" Depression can range from mild and temporary to debilitating and long lasting.

The final stage is acceptance. "This firing happened and there is nothing I can do to change it. I need to figure things out, get on with my life and find another job."

These emotional reactions do not always come in the exact order above, although that is a common path for the grief rollercoaster. Regardless, no one is immune from experiencing some or all of these stages. After all, we are human beings and the thing that unites us is our ability to feel.

When I am looking at this from the corporate perspective—as a Chief Communications Officer—it helps me to know that our staff can experience the five stages of grief during a tumultuous time. Knowing this enables me to better guide the CEO in her or his communications with the employees. It also informs me about how to better interact with my own department staff.

I find it comforting to know that we all process loss in a similar way. Whoever we are communicating with during a crisis, it is important for us to be mindful of the emotional state of the people we are talking to and what they could be experiencing.

CHAPTER 4 | MESSAGE & TONE IN COMMUNICATIONS

In the last couple of chapters, we covered two key themes: (1) how the human brain responds to stress and change and (2) the emotional and behavioral reactions we exhibit during those periods. Therefore, you now have a pretty good understanding of core human reactions to change and stress. This should set you up to better implement the crisis communications strategies used by PR professionals.

My 30 years as a public relations executive have included innumerable crises. I have had a front-row seat as the corporate drama unfolds and I have witnessed how to handle crisis communications well and how to seriously mess it up. I do not know a single PR person who walks into a crisis and says to themselves, "I think I will intentionally try to make this worse." Unfortunately, intentions do not always translate well to good crisis management.

When I think about how to best deliver a message in a way that I can influence thought and behavior, I am doing it from two perspectives. The first is obviously as a PR person with a long career communicating with various constituents. The second is from a psychological perspective. I consider how human beings react to fear and change, and then I think about how to say something in a way that they will be able to hear.

In a crisis, the person who is the most respected and believable is the person who speaks calmly with authority, but not in an authoritarian way. PR professionals include several key elements in a crisis response.

The message and tone of the speaker should be...

1. Timely
2. Transparent } MESSAGE
3. Truthful

4. Clear
5. Confident } TONE
6. Compassionate

Timely, transparent and truthful are about your message. Calm, confident and compassionate have to do with your tone. Obviously, confidence and compassion are also transmitted through your message.

Combine these with what you now know about stress and emotional reactions from the SCARF and Kübler-Ross models. You now have a powerful structure for speaking to others during a crisis.

Contrary to the anecdotes I used to open this book, some good examples of effective crisis communications did happen during the COVID-19 pandemic. In the Introduction, I mentioned the skilled communications style of Dr. Anthony Fauci, who became America's most crushed-on doctor during the pandemic when residents of several U.S. states were under "stay in place" orders.[25] Similarly, New York Governor Andrew Cuomo gained nationwide attention and admiration for his leadership and calm, clear communications style. *New York Times* writer Ben Smith penned a column with the headline, "Andrew Cuomo Is the Control Freak We Need Right Now."[26] Rebecca Fishbein, a contributor to the feminist website Jezebel.com, wrote a humorous story about developing a crush on Cuomo from the captivity of her apartment. She stated, "I am lonely and scared and anxious, but I have mitigated some of these feelings with my day's two bright spots: 1) My afternoon run, and 2) New York Governor Andrew Cuomo's daily streamed press conference."[27]

During the COVID-19 crisis, Governor Cuomo held daily press briefings, which were carried live on many TV networks, as well as on the Governor's official website and Facebook page. He began all of his briefings with the facts. He was measured and calm as he reported the rising numbers of cases and deaths in New York State, which at one point had 10 times as many cases as any other state in the nation. He reported uncomfortable facts about the lack of hospital beds, as well as ventilators—7,000 procured and 30,000 needed.[28] He was transparent about the conversations he was having with private companies and the federal government in trying to get the equipment and funding. He stated all of it clearly and simply, while providing reassurance, "We will get through this. ... We are New York tough."[29]

More importantly, Governor Cuomo showed his humanity and sympathy. Before taking reporters' questions, Cuomo ended every briefing with his personal opinion, which he made clear was his personal opinion and not fact. He talked about his feelings and said he was inspired by the retired medical practitioners and mental health professionals—some from other states—who volunteered to come back to work and help New York. He provided uplifting quotes, such as, "This situation is not easy. But easy times don't forge character. It's the tough times that forge character."[30]

If you apply SCARF, people's certainty and autonomy were taken away. If you also consider Kübler-Ross' theory of grief, New Yorkers were grieving the loss of their everyday lives. Cuomo recognized that the public's emotions were high. His daily briefings reframed all of the negative news with solid facts, while also providing assurances to deal with the emotional reactions.

Not everyone will love a politician, no matter what he or she does. Cuomo still had his detractors, but during the daily live briefings, the Facebook comments from constituents made it clear that many of those who disliked him and disagreed with his politics could at least admit that he was showing good leadership and they respected how he was guiding New York State through the crisis.

If It's That Easy, Why Can't Everybody Do It?

What Cuomo did seems like a simple thing, but just because something is simple, does not mean it is easy.

It is almost impossible to find a comprehensive definition of crisis communications. Following is the one I use when teaching my graduate-level students at Columbia University. It comes from the Business Dictionary, which is an online resource.

It defines crisis communications in business as: "The effort taken by a company to communicate with the public and stockholders when an unexpected event occurs that could have a negative impact on the company's reputation. This can also refer to the efforts of business or governmental entities to inform employees or the public of a potential hazard such as an impending storm which could have a catastrophic impact."[31]

There are real costs and tangible effects to mismanaging a crisis. People can die or they experience mental, emotional and other physical harm. For organizations, brand reputation can suffer, product sales can go down, the value of the company can drop, and people can lose their jobs. Not every crisis is a disaster; however, even small events can turn into bigger problems for governments, companies and individuals if they are not managed properly.

This is why it is important to remain calm in a crisis and be mindful of the tools at your disposal. It helps influence others as you navigate those big changes.

Admittedly, the British may have cornered the market on this concept with their popular and much-appropriated motto, "Keep calm and carry on." I wish I could come up with something as pithy and memorable to help retrain your brain during a crisis. I look forward to people sending me suggestions, because the best I could come up with while writing this is: "Think in slo-mo and speak like Cuomo."

Before you throw tomatoes at me through your e-book reader, remember that jingles can be very helpful for remembering concepts! To this day, many of us still use the phrase "Be Like Mike" to motivate us when we are trying to master a skill. For those of you who are too young to know that slogan, "Be Like Mike" was a popular ad campaign from sports drink manufacturer Gatorade in 1992.[32] It featured kids aspiring to play basketball like Michael Jordan, who had just won his first championship with the Chicago Bulls.

CHAPTER 5 | METHOD & MEDIUM IN COMMUNICATIONS

You can have the best message in the world, but you still need to be able to reach the people. That is where the medium comes into play—<u>where</u> you communicate is as important as <u>what</u> you communicate.

The only way to reach people is to go where they are. That can be a huge challenge in today's world. It has never been easier to communicate, but that accessibility means endless fragmentation of news and information. Infinite accessibility also means there is a huge amount of noise, which makes it hard for people to spend a significant amount of time paying attention to the messages that do reach them.

So, to get people to see your message and to absorb it, you need to speak in a language they understand in a place where they will see it. I am not just talking about translating your message into foreign languages, although that could also be vital, depending on whom you need to reach.

The way you speak to a 70-year-old and where you place that message is very different from the way you speak to a 17-year-old and where you place that message. At the start of the book, I illustrated this problem with the example of what happened in the United States when the COVID-19 crisis began and young people appeared not to be taking the threat seriously.

They were ignoring official warnings to socially distance by going to the beach during spring break, packing bars at night and playing contact sports in the parks during the day. It took officials a few weeks to realize that they were not communicating with America's youth on key platforms, like TikTok, Snapchat and Instagram. In addition, they were not using young peers to convey the information.

I would also argue that the officials and politicians were using the wrong words. They were telling people to practice social distancing. Nobody was social distancing during the COVID-19 lockdown, because in the digital era, people were connected by video calls, social media and telephone. The youth needed to be told to <u>physically distance</u> but continue to <u>socially connect</u>. That would have been a better way to communicate what was happening—with the added bonus of helping soothe people living with a lot of uncertainty (remember that certainty is the "C" in SCARF).

This was a perfect example of why the medium that you use to transmit your message is as important as the message.

If you want to speak to the Silent Generation (born 1928-1945) and Baby Boomers (1946-1964)[33] in the U.S., a business leader, politician, and government official is the key messenger. A newspaper, cable news channel or broadcast news outlet is the best medium. *The Wall Street Journal, The New York Times, USA Today,* the Associated Press, Reuters, NPR, CNN, Fox News Channel, as well as ABC, CBS and NBC's nightly newscasts are still the way to reach the older generations.

If you want to speak to Generation X (1965-1980)[34] or older Millennials (those born in the 1980s), that same leader or official may be the right messenger, but make sure your message is being carried in popular blogs, online publications, and aggregator news sites like *Huffington Post, BuzzFeed, Refinery29, Fast Company, Axios, Drudge Report,* Google News, Yahoo News, and the Apple News App. Also, the message should be transmitted by zeitgeisty talk show hosts, such as John Oliver, Trevor Noah, Jimmy Kimmel, Stephen Colbert and Seth Meyers. When Bill Gates wanted to outline his philanthropical approach to helping world governments with COVID-19, he went on *The Daily Show with Trevor Noah*, not *60 Minutes*—the stalwart newsmagazine that used to be the go-to outlet for a deep dive into timely and important issues.

When you need to reach younger Millennials (those born in the early to mid-1990s) and Gen Z, disregard everything above. The most trusted source of information for them is word of mouth, whether it be family and friends or micro influencers (defined as having around 50,000 social media followers).[35] The best place to reach this group is on Instagram, TikTok, Snapchat, YouTube and Reddit. Traditional publishers, like Condé Nast, Hearst and Meredith have gotten very good at reaching today's youth, but they are doing it with video content that is completely different from what you see in the pages of their magazines. They are making short video series—some are influencer-driven, and others are topic-driven—but all are entertaining and aimed at speaking to Americans under 30 years old.

Best Practices from My Crisis Communications Handbook

Besides communications, there are some best practices for managing a crisis, whether you are a government entity, private company or an individual dealing with a friend or family member. These communications tools are not just for big companies and big government, they are for everybody.

What follows is a broad list of general practices that communications professionals follow during a corporate crisis. Think of this list as a guideline that you can use to fill in the specifics in your given situation.

Know When to Stop Business as Usual

This includes everything from carefully considering when a government needs to quarantine a city, when a company needs to recall a product, or when a family needs to intervene on a member who is drinking too much or could be a harm to themselves or others.

Find Ways to Show That You Care

Whether you are a company, a government entity or an individual, this practice is not just about words; it is also about actions. During the COVID-19 pandemic, big companies all over the world stopped making their own products in order to manufacture hand sanitizer, surgical masks and ventilators, all of which were in short supply. Government officials dropped partisanship and worked together to enact a relief package for U.S. citizens. Individual medical and mental health professionals came out of retirement and offered their services to help an overflowing health care system.

Get Out in Front of the Information

Do not let the media, competition or rumor mill control the agenda. This is about using the six tenets of crisis communications. Timely, transparent and truthful communications said in a clear, confident and compassionate way.

Delays Do More Harm Than Good

Even the slightest delay in communicating can harm your credibility and your organization's reputation. As the saying goes, nature abhors a vacuum. Silence during a crisis leads people to fill the void, which propagates speculation, misinformation and general distrust.

Operate with Purpose

Develop messages and do all planning with a clear goal in mind. Whether your goal is to get the economy back on track, get a company up and running or get life back to normal for you and your family, make every decision in a smart, measured way that always keeps your ultimate goal in mind.

Pay Attention to Rumors

When you hear rumors around the crisis, work to eliminate them. As we say in my industry, "Shut that shit down!" (Pardon the profanity, but it is a popular saying because of the alliteration with the word sh*t.)

When we were kids, there was a game called telephone. You sat on the floor with 10 or more of your closest friends and the first person whispered a message to the person sitting next to them. Then that person whispered the message to the person next to them, and so on and so on, until you got to the end of the chain. The person at the end announced the message—the way they heard it—and it was ALWAYS WRONG. It never failed that, during the chain of communication, the message had been completely butchered. [The amusing twist here is that something we thought was funny as kids turned into a major annoyance as adults.]

Rumors do the same in a crisis. Nip them in the bud. Rumors are like a festering fungus that rot a system from the inside out, so squash them quickly.

Question Everything!

During a crisis, no question is too stupid, too naïve, too inconsequential. You never know what question will lead to a huge AHA! moment.

A friend of mine was the head of PR for a regional airline that was struggling and ended up in Chapter 11 bankruptcy. The airline had worked out a new contract with the pilot's union during Chapter 11, but there was an unexpected work slowdown by the union members. A lot of pilots were calling in sick, flights were being canceled and passengers were angry. The CEO of the company was ready to declare an all-out-war with the pilot's union and take them to court.

During a late-night crisis strategy session, the head of PR said to the core team assembled, "Does anyone know why the pilots are staging a sick out?" None of the executives in the room could answer the question. After a few phone calls, the CEO learned that the pilots had objected to language in the Chapter 11 deal, which said they could be forced to work for three days straight with no sleep. Well, nobody wanted that. It would be dangerous! For whatever reason, the problem had not been adequately communicated to airline higher ups and the CEO instantly ordered the company's lawyers to file an amended legal agreement with the bankruptcy court. The pilots went back to work immediately.

What Not to Do

These are all good tools for how to communicate during a crisis, but I think it is equally important to share some helpful tips about what NOT to do in a crisis.

Do NOT Ignore Potential Problems

Many crises begin with an avoidable problem that someone, or even a group of people, recognized as being a threat well before it became a crisis. While it is impractical and impossible to go through life anticipating and avoiding every conceivable risk, it is helpful to have some paranoia about those issues that can snowball, whether it is in your personal or professional life. Avoiding the problem, pooh-poohing it, and/or denying the severity of it just puts you behind the eight ball when things get really bad (those who play billiards know that the worst position on a pool table is trapped behind the eight ball).

Do NOT Be Dishonest

Lying, telling only partial truths and/or being misleading will get you in more hot water. When it is revealed that you have been dishonest or misleading, your credibility is shot, people will not believe what you are saying, and it makes a stressful problem worse for you.

Do NOT Blame Others

Blaming and shaming never work. In Japan, when people bring shame on themselves and their families, it causes deep humiliation and some even kill themselves over it.[36] In the United States, when we are publicly shamed, our cultural practice is to become defensive and angry. This is how we have been culturally conditioned. So, when you blame someone else, especially if you do it publicly, it turns into a fight with finger pointing and name calling. It is not a unifying or productive way to solve a crisis.

Do NOT Over Confess

Crisis communications is not meant to be like the old practice of Confession in the Catholic Church. Think of it this way: If you have ever had a significant other cheat on you, when they come clean about it, it is hard enough to hear the facts. If he or she then shares more details about the affair than just the basic facts, you know how painful that is. It is like burning an image in your mind that you cannot erase.

In a crisis—whether it is personal or professional—be transparent and truthful, be factual and sympathetic, but do not overshare. This is why it is so important to try to stay calm, so the amygdala does not hijack your brain. You want executive functioning, rational thinking, and self-control to be online and fully functional. With the amygdala running the show, every childhood episode we had where we spilled our guts and felt better afterwards will come into play and that is not a helpful way to communicate in a crisis.

41

CHAPTER 6 | COMMUNICATIONS ≠ INFLUENCE

I t is obviously helpful to be able to communicate clearly and effectively in a crisis. Message and tone coupled with the method and medium are a vital part of the equation. However, you also have to be able to influence people to take an action, change their behavior or just plain listen to reason!

Many people assume that just because they say something, others will listen. That is not true. If it were true, people would abide by every corporate or political directive during a crisis. Influence comes from more than just words in a statement.

If you go to Barnes & Noble or Amazon, you will find myriad books about how to influence people. There is a classic book by businessman Dale Carnegie, *How to Win Friends & Influence People,* first published in 1936, that is still popular today. There are also modern business books, including *How to Influence People* by John C. Maxwell and Jim Dornan, published in 2013, and *Persuasion: The Art of Influencing People* by James Borg, published in 2009.

Each of the books has its own device for presenting the material. For example, Maxwell and Dornan use the word INFLUENCER as an acronym to help remember the principles they teach.[37] Carnegie presents his ideas in an organized list form. Not surprisingly, nearly all books about how to influence people are saying the same thing, which is to listen to other people, understand where they are coming from, empower them to make decisions and do not be critical of them.

When it comes to influencing people, we are talking about human nature and that does not change. Yes, it is true that times change and society modernizes. Fads go in and out. But what does not change is our basic human drives.

There is a critical distinction here—the difference between how it feels to us when we are attacked, versus when we are understood. A crisis by all outward appearances may not be a crisis to the amygdala if a person feels that he or she is being understood, versus attacked. This is neuroscience and there are a lot of factors involved, but the amygdala is the primary brain center responsible for governing how we react to one another.

As a PR executive, I believe in clarity and simplicity. Frankly, I believe that about all communications—whether I am in my role as a corporate spokesperson or I am speaking to a group while wearing my psychology hat. Influencing people does not need to be complex.

That is why I have boiled it down into three easy steps:

1. Understand where someone is coming from
2. Compliment and relate to them
3. Give them a choice and empower them to make their own decision

1ST—Understand Where They Are Coming From

Understanding people makes YOU more effective at dealing with differences. It is also helpful to the other person, because when we feel understood, our defenses go down, we are more open to different ideas, and we are more open to making a change.

What is the trick to understanding people? This one is simple. Stop assuming the worst about someone and what they have said or done. ASK them about it and be open to their rationale.

- Ask what they mean by what they said.
- Ask why they took the action they took.
- Be genuinely curious about who they are as a person and what makes them tick.

Also, listen to what they are saying when they answer your question. Do not do that thing where you are formulating your own response in your mind and not really listening to what the person is saying.

This is also one of those simple but not easy concepts, because what do you do if you think that the person said or did something that is vile, unconscionable and unacceptable? If you ask why from curiosity, as opposed to asking it from a place of anger and aggression, you will elicit an answer that helps you understand the person better. When you understand them better, you can be more influential.

Understanding where people are coming from can also include thinking about their emotional and behavioral reactions to fear. Yes, I am bringing us back to SCARF and Kübler-Ross' five stages of grief. All of the tools I present in this book can be used fluidly and interchangeably.

Helpful Hint

Watch your tone. People are not stupid. We can all hear it when you ask a question that is followed by the silent, "You moron!" Being sarcastic only gets you into a snark fest. So, when you ask your question, do not phrase it in a condescending way, such as...

"WHAT were you thinking?!"
"What did you mean by THAT?!"

Being combative only makes the other person defensive and angry. Then they dig into their belief system deeper. It helps if you ask from genuine curiosity as opposed to asking in a way that puts people on the defensive. I will give you a perfect example of how not to ask a question—unless you are a reporter and you are intentionally trying to be inflammatory.

During the COVID-19 crisis, Governor Cuomo was holding his live daily press briefing when Jesse McKinley, Albany Bureau Chief for the New York Times, asked the Governor, "Considering how far off the [*hospital*] bed projections have been, do you worry about your credibility in warning people about what might have come… might be coming? Does that affect your credibility?"[38]

Cuomo's response was measured, but defensive. "Because I relied on experts who were making a projection?" he asked. "No. I think my credibility would be affected if I didn't ask experts for their opinion and then do everything I can to meet those numbers that they produced."

The Governor then defended the experts that the State of New York worked with during the COVID-19 crisis, which included Columbia University, Weill Cornell, and McKinsey & Company, among others. "You ask the best minds for what you should be prepared for and then you do everything you can to meet those numbers. The way you lose credibility is either you're in denial about what you're looking at, or you don't act fast enough, or you don't achieve the goal. That's how you lose credibility in these situations. … My job is to prepare for the worst; hope for the best."

The Governor was put on the defensive with his answer. The truth is that the projections were likely right, and the reason they never got to the higher numbers is because the actions that New York took successfully flattened the curve of the projections.

Fortunately, this interaction happened during a press conference that went for almost an hour. The Governor moved on to the next reporter's question, which one of his deputy's answered. That gave Cuomo the chance to reassess his answer to McKinley. Before the next reporter's question, Cuomo jumped in and said, "Excuse me one second, because I gave Jesse only half an answer. What the statisticians will say is they were right. They said we could flatten the curve if we took certain actions and if people complied with those actions. They will say that's why the curve is flatter."

Governor Cuomo then got in his own slight dig coupled with a compliment of the reporter, "Your rejoinder would have to be, as a provocative journalist, 'Well how do you know it would have hit your projection?' And they'll say, 'I believe it would have. Had you not done the closedown—the New York pause. Had you not been so diligent on compliance. We believe the infection rate would have hit our model. It did not hit our model because of the New York pause and the compliance, etc.'"

Because the person at the podium always has the final word, the Governor ended his response to McKinley by saying that the question was essentially unanswerable, "Well, if none of those policies were put in place, would you have hit those numbers [*the modeled projections*]? Nobody will ever know."

The reporter's question was phrased provocatively and it put the Governor on the defensive. His initial response was to dig in and to defend himself. Because Governor Cuomo had a few minutes to think about it and revisit the answer, he was able to give the factually based, accurate answer, as opposed to his initial non-factual, more emotionally defensive response.

Had McKinley asked his question in a different way, a way that came from genuine curiosity, as opposed to one that assumed to know the answer (that the Governor's credibility had been hurt), it might have sounded like this, "Governor, the consultants projected that New York could need as many as 170,000 hospital beds to treat COVID-19 patients and so far we have needed far less than that. Can you help us understand the difference between the projections and the reality?"

After spending 30 years working with journalists—and having been married to one in the 1990s and early 2000s—I can tell you that reporters are often intentionally needling (regardless of whether or not they are your spouse). Journalists are trained to ask questions in a way that will elicit an incendiary response. It is an effective tactic, if you are a reporter. It is not an effective tactic if you are trying to influence people.

Food for Thought

With each of the three principles on how to influence people, try it out on yourself to get more insight into why this works. How do you react when someone asks you something in an aggressive way? You may feel shame and embarrassment. You could feel fear for having done something wrong or bad. But in order to protect us, our egos often turn feelings of weakness into anger. Anger is strength. But anger also creates rigidity in our belief system.

Ask yourself honestly, how would I react if someone in my life—a parent, sibling, friend, boss or colleague—asked me…

"HOW could you think like that?!"
"WHY would you say something like that?!"
"So, how is THAT working for you?!"

2ND—Compliment & Relate to Them

Jimmy Durante famously said, "Be nice to people on your way up because you meet them on your way down."

Being able to influence people is primarily about how those people view you. Three key components are:

1. I believe you.
2. I respect you.
3. I feel safe, e.g., I trust you.

It is important to note that respect is not about being liked. In this case, respect is about trust and feeling safe. Remember, the amygdala kicks in during a crisis and shuts down executive functioning. When it does that, rational thinking and decision making fly out the window as the amygdala searches the memory banks for anything that calms down the system. In that moment, the amygdala is searching for SAFETY. The safety of the organism is its primary job.

In order to influence friends, family, colleagues or nations during a crisis, people need to believe what you are saying to them and they need to think that you are leading them to safety.

Influencing is an art, but it is one we are all capable of when we use the tools. Compliment, praise and/or relate to people. Do not shame, blame or criticize. Remember the old English adage, "You catch more flies with honey than with vinegar."[39]

If being sweet instead of a bit salty does not come naturally to you, or feels like it is not genuine for you, then think about it from the perspective of the SCARF method. When someone's status is threatened, the fix is to praise them publicly. Similarly, when someone is angry (which is one of the five stages of grief in Kübler-Ross' theory), pointing out what they do well or relating to them in some way, defuses the situation.

Helpful Hint

So far, I have covered two of the three components to influencing people:

1. Understand where someone is coming from
2. Then compliment and relate to them

I find that real-world examples are helpful for explaining these concepts. So, for this next example, I am going to stay with the COVID-19 theme, since it was such a big crisis in the United States and worldwide at the time this book was written.

I was in my local grocery store during the height of the pandemic in New York City, when we were mandated to wear face masks. An older woman, who was wearing her mask down around her chin (as opposed to covering her nose and mouth), coughed in the aisle as I walked by her.

I instantly jumped on her and said, "Mam, put your mask on! You're coughing and it's dangerous."

My response was from fear and stress, because my amygdala had kicked in, since my brain thought I was in danger of catching the virus. My comment was an attack, so the woman's response was predictable.

"I have allergies," she said defensively as she started to head down a different aisle in the store.

I quickly shot back at her, "I know, but it is still dangerous. You should be wearing your mask!"

First of all, I did not know she had allergies. How could I possibly know that? Second, it was a completely ineffective way of trying to get her to wear her mask. All she did was roll her eyes and walk away with her mask still dangling around her chin.

This is a perfect example of what happens when we blame, shame and publicly humiliate someone. If you think about the SCARF method, my sense of **fairness** was activated. New Yorkers were under an executive order to wear masks, so everyone should have been wearing them in public (fairness).

Because I was worried about my safety, I was also clearly in fight, flight or freeze mode. Had my rational brain been in control, I might have paused and asked her why she was not wearing her mask. If I had been inquisitive as opposed to accusatory, the exchange might have been more productive.

If you think about the six tenets of crisis communications from the earlier chapter, my message was timely, transparent and truthful, but I did not convey calm, confident and compassionate. You can have the right message, but if your tone is punitive, your message will not be well received.

Using the art of influencing others, following is how the conversation could have worked: The first thing I needed to do was **understand** why the woman was not wearing the mask around her nose and mouth. The best way to do that would have been to ask the question. Remember, it is important to be genuinely curious about the person's answer.

Let us pretend that I asked nicely, "I noticed you're wearing your mask differently. Would you tell me why? I am constantly tugging at mine and I am curious about how you are wearing yours."

This is a kinder way of approaching the conversation. I am also relating to her. The masks were awkward for those who were not used to wearing them.

The woman's response to me then may have been, "I have allergies and it is really hard for me to breathe through this mask. It makes my allergies worse."

Once I understood the woman's perspective, I could have used that information to **compliment and/or relate**

to her. "That makes a lot of sense. I understand where you're coming from. I find it really hard to breathe through the mask, as well. It also smells kind of funny, which makes me not want to wear it."

Now, I have teed up the woman to be influenced. The tone and phrasing of my response is going to be much better received than one that sounds nagging, authoritative or punitive.

Take this conversation and apply it to conversations you have in your professional life. Even if you are the boss, when you interact with coworkers and your staff in a way that is bossy, authoritarian and officious, you are less influential.

If you are not sure that is true, then meditate on it for a minute (that is my way of saying think about it). Are you frustrated by the way people respond to you? Are you frustrated about the way work gets done or by the amount of time it takes to get it done? Consider how you speak to your staff, coworkers or kids, and try implementing these tools for how to influence others.

Food for Thought

Blaming and shaming do not work, especially when you do it in front of other people! Humiliating someone or making them look bad will get their defense mechanisms up and armed quickly. If you need proof, just go on Twitter. It is easy to lob a mean critique over a digital fence at someone you do not know and will never meet while you sit safely in your own home.

It is true that aggressive, angry, mean people get ahead in life. But they leave a lot of destruction in their path and the fall from the top of the mountain they have built is often humbling and humiliating. In today's world, the old saying that nice guys finish last is a fallacy.

Young adults, who comprise Millennials and Generation Z, have helped shepherd a new feelings-based management style into the workforce. It is a more "woke" way of treating each other. Those of us who have been in business for several decades know that it did not used to be that way. Older workers came up the ranks during a time when the workplace was a dictatorship, not a democracy. WHATEVER the boss said is what you did. HOW the boss said it is just how he or she said it.

There was less concern for people's feelings. In fact, in my early 20s, I was specifically told by a mentor not to bring my feelings to work. Older workers, who comprise the Silent Generation and Baby Boomers, have a hard time adjusting to the more feelings-based management style required by Millennial and Gen Z workers.

Interestingly, Generation X is more open to the changes being brought by younger generations. Their adaptability has to do with the psychographics of Gen X, which has been nicknamed America's middle child because it is a small generation sandwiched between two very large cohorts—the Boomers and Millennials.

Today's parents have also taught their progeny to be more mindful about their actions and how they affect the environment, other animals, and especially other human beings. Younger generations have been raised with more awareness than prior generations. In my mind, that is a good thing.

People who continue to sow derision and divisiveness—whether it be politicians, business leaders, celebrities, media pundits or your Uncle Bob—will find that old ways are changing as younger Millennials and Gen Z come into power in business and politics. These generations know and respect the idea that intolerance met by intolerance only leads to more intolerance.

3RD—Empower Them to Make Their Own Decision

In order for people to do what you want them to do, they actually have to want to do it.

That is a brain teaser, so let me phrase it more simply. People have to want to do something in order to do it.

Here is a surefire way to remember it. Animals have to want to do something in order for us to get them to do it. Ergo the saying, "You can lead a horse to water, but you can't make him drink." Think about how dogs react the minute they realize they are about to enter the vet's office. Front paws go out, butts go down, and all of their weight and effort goes into NOT moving. The human being taking the dog to the vet always wins but, depending on the size of the dog, it can be quite a struggle, which results in a lot of funny videos on social media.

I use these two examples to drive home the idea that people are the same. There is an axiom, "The mind rejects that which it does not seek."

How many parents throw their hands up in frustration when they try to get their toddler, teen or twentysomething kid to do what they say? Business is no different. Many managers know that being a good boss is not about being bossy. In fact, the most effective leaders inspire their employees to want to succeed and empower them to do it themselves.

Influencing people is about speaking with authority, but not being authoritarian. That is why the third step in how to influence people during a crisis is about empowering others to make their own decisions.

It is a simple concept that is not easy to do. Think back to the six tenets of crisis communications—timely, transparent, truthful, clear, confident, compassionate.

Whether you are talking one-on-one or to a large group of people, being truthful and transparent means that you are empowering people with facts.

Being clear with them and providing them the information in a timely manner means that you are empowering them to make critical decisions of their own.

Delivering your message with confidence and compassion means you are empowering them to be clearheaded and make rational decisions from a place of calm, as opposed to being angry, scared or feeling attacked.

Furthermore, all of this is true whether you consider it from the perspective of the six key tenets of crisis communications, the SCARF model or the five stages of grief theory.

Helpful Hint

I grew up in New York City and moved to Los Angeles when I was 18 years old to attend the University of Southern California (USC). After college, I went to work at the international PR firm Fleishman Hillard and, a few years later, I landed a great job at CBS as a senior publicist. At that point, I had been living in LA for nearly 10 years and I had mostly acclimated to the friendlier, more relaxed way of being... or so I thought.

One afternoon, I was sitting at my desk in CBS's LA office when I got a phone call from Ann Morfogen, the head of the PR department, who was based in NYC. Ann had recently announced she was leaving the company and she called to say goodbye. It was a nice phone call, but I was surprised when she called me. I was relatively junior, did not report directly to her and, most importantly, Ann had never called me before then.

The conversation was brief, because she had only one reason for calling—she wanted to help me, and she said something I will never forget. "Joanna, you're really good at your job. You're going to go far, which is why I want to tell you something. You've got to lose the New York attitude. You don't need it to succeed and it could hurt you."

Some of us are naturally good at inspiring people and making them feel safe and others of us are not. That was 25 years ago, and I took to heart what Ann said. I have worked hard to communicate with people in a way that is respectful and calm. I am not perfect at it. You can take the girl out of New York, but you cannot take the New York out of the girl! That means I have failed at it plenty of times, although, experience and age have definitely helped refine it.

The process I have outlined in this chapter for how to influence people may sound like an annoying task to some of you. The three steps, which include understanding people, complimenting and relating to them, and then empowering them to make their own decisions, do not come naturally for all of us. If you are one of those people, I have a game for you to play that will help you be more influential.

The famous Greek philosopher, Socrates, developed a method of inquiry that we now call Socratic questioning. The teacher asks questions of the student that help the student test the validity of his or her ideas. A key component of Socratic questioning is that the teacher (a.k.a., authority figure) comes at the line of questioning from a position of not knowing the answer.[40] This is a vital part of the method. Why? Because when we think we know the right answer, we lose the opportunity to influence the person who is answering the questions.

I use the Socratic method a lot with the women I mentor and it is very effective at influencing them without me actually telling them what I think they "should do." Let me demonstrate the method using my awkward exchange in the grocery store with the older woman whom I had snapped at for not wearing her face mask correctly.

In Step 2: Compliment & Relate to Them, I said that the woman would probably be more open to the idea that she should wear a face mask properly, if I had: (1) stopped to understand her rationale for wearing it around her chin, and (2) then related to her, since I also thought the masks were uncomfortable.

Now it is time for me to deploy Step 3: Empowering Others to Make Their Own Decision. Below is an example of how I could have applied Socratic questioning with the lady in the grocery store. You will recall that, in the fictitious version of our conversation, she told me that the mask was irritating her allergies and I said I related to how uncomfortable breathing is while wearing the mask.

> *Me:* "I struggle with the discomfort of the mask versus the directive that everyone should wear masks. I have heard that 25 percent of people are asymptomatic and transmit the virus without knowing it. Are you worried about getting sick?"

> *Woman:* "I keep a safe distance from people, and I don't have a choice. I really can't breathe well with these allergies now that it is springtime."

> *Me:* "That's a conundrum. I can't breathe well in it and I don't have allergies! Since we have been asked to wear masks for the good of everyone, do you think it is worthwhile to wear one in order to help alleviate other people's discomfort? As a show of solidarity?"

> *Woman:* "Yes, that's a good way of looking at it, but I can't wear this thing for more than a few minutes."

> *Me:* "The health officials have also said people can wear scarves, bandanas and other items around their nose and mouth to act as protection when they're outside. Do you have anything that you would feel comfortable wearing that would also help show solidarity with your fellow New Yorkers?"

Woman: "I do have a lovely collection of scarves. I've never worn them around my mouth and nose like a bandit, but I think that it makes sense to do for other people's comfort."

Notice that I never had to give my personal opinion on whether or not she should cover her nose and mouth with the mask. The purpose of Socratic questioning is to empower the person to come to their own conclusion through questioning, not lecturing.

Food for Thought

When I talk about these concepts, people sometimes assume that I am saying they should not disagree with others, or even have an opinion. That is not at all what I am saying. You can disagree with people, but do not tell them they are wrong. It is that old adage, "You can't win an argument, so don't get in one."

When we criticize people, blame them or publicly shame them, we are setting up a dynamic that guarantees they will become defensive and more anchored in their belief system. We are guaranteeing that we cannot win the argument.

Again, if you need proof of this, look at Twitter. We are not winning any converts to our way of thinking when we make fun of people who believe differently than we do and call them names, like we did when we were kids on the playground. I have seen friends spew nasty things on Facebook and Twitter about U.S. politicians, but turn around and scold their kids for calling each other names and throwing sand in the sandbox—without any self-awareness about the contradiction in what they just did.

Intolerance met by intolerance just leads to more intolerance. It does not lead to influencing and leading others during a crisis—or at any other time, for that matter.

CHAPTER 7 | THE RULES OF LIFE ACCORDING TO...

Russian author Leo Tolstoy (1828-1910) said, "Everyone thinks of changing the world, but no one thinks of changing himself."[41]

The truth about communicating during a crisis—or communicating period—is that we do not see the world as is it, we see the world as we are.[42] That is a rewording of a heady quote by author Anaïs Nin (1903-1977).

So, what did Anaïs Nin mean? Let me unpack that, because it is a psychological reality that most of us do not consider as we go about our daily lives.

As I said in an earlier chapter, everyone has written a book in their mind, *The Rules of Life According to Me*. Human beings have an internal rule book, which includes our ideas about what behaviors are acceptable and not acceptable; the things we like and do not like; and what we want and do not want.

The interesting thing about this rule book is that we did not make the rules, nor did we choose them. Our beliefs come from our human conditioning, most of which happens in childhood. Everything that occurs in life contributes to our conditioning. Our personal belief system is formed by our parents' views and those of our parents' parents; the religion we practice (or do not practice); the schools we attend; the city, state and country in which we live; the era in which we grow up; and the language we speak; to name a few. All of this affects who we are and how we think. The really interesting part is *we do not consciously choose any of it*, because we are born into it.

More importantly, *The Rules of Life According to Me* dictates how we think and feel about *everything*. For example, when I see a Christmas tree, it brings up feelings of joy and warmth. My father made a huge deal about Christmas; it was a magical time for me growing up. My friend Diana grew up in a violent household. Her parents fought a lot and, when Diana was nine years old, the Christmas tree was used as a weapon during a fight and it ended up at the bottom of the basement stairs. It is a traumatic memory for Diana. When she sees a Christmas tree, she feels a mixture of intense emotions, including sadness, anxiety and anger.

A tree is just a tree; in and of itself, it is neutral. But it means something different to Diana than it does to me because of our subjective experiences in life. We cannot see something as simple as a tree without having a preconceived judgment of what it means. This is true of everything in life. As human beings, we do not experience *anything* without having a subjective experience of it.

I believe it is an important sentiment to end with, because we can do everything flawlessly and things still do not work out the way we want or think they should. And that is okay, because *The Rules of Life According to Me* is a fictional novel anyway.

Cultivate a Shared Understanding

One of the most important things about crisis communications done right is that it allows everybody to have a shared understanding of the situation. However, as television channels have multiplied, blogs have become as influential as newspapers, social media has become ubiquitous, and everything in life has become more fragmented, we have less of a shared understanding of anything.

We live in our own information bubble and have the ability to discard (literally delete) other perspectives, if we even see them at all. Our digital world is like an echo chamber for our own beliefs, morals and politics. We obtain our information and content from search engines, such as Google; social media platforms, like Facebook; and recommendation sites, ala Amazon. But these digital services rely on algorithms that serve up information they think we want based on our digital footprint, i.e., our prior digital behavior. When we ask a search engine a question, it is not giving us an objective answer, it gives us the answer by providing it from sources it knows we like.

Given all of that, it is not surprising that the United States is experiencing a culture clash the likes of which it has not seen since the hippie counterculture movement in the 1960s and 1970s. The differences are not just along ideological lines. Many of the miscommunications and misunderstandings happen between the older and younger generations. This can get especially complicated at work, where we have five generations in the workforce for the first time ever.

The Silent Generation, Baby Boomers and Generation X had accepted a way of life where information flowed from the top like a corporate pyramid or a military style operation. Politicians, business leaders and celebrities were the primary voices in the news. The newspapers, radio talk shows and TV newscasts were the gatekeepers who dictated what information made it to the public.

Today, we communicate peer-to-peer across an infinite number of digital channels. It is the great equalizer. Everyone has a voice and their message can be amplified to millions of people around the world.

If I were to summarize this whole book into one cogent message, it would be that its entire point is to find a shared understanding so we can work together in a crisis. What I hope you gained from it are tools for how to do that despite the deep fragmentation that exists now and for the foreseeable future.

J oanna Dodd Massey is an experienced C-level communications executive and Board Director, who advises executive teams at Fortune 500 companies, startups and nonprofits. She has worked for over 25 years strategizing on global brand reputation management at companies, such as Condé Nast, Lionsgate, CBS, Viacom, Discovery and Hasbro. She managed corporate turnaround as Condé Nast transitioned from print to digital video; risk and crisis communications for publicly held companies with their consumers, regulators, investors and advertisers; culture transformation when Lionsgate purchased Starz, CBS converted UPN to The CW, and Discovery shuttered its Hub TV Network; successful communications with diverse stakeholders as head of internal and external communications; and multi-million-dollar P&Ls as a department leader. Dr. Massey's career spans media, film, TV, digital video, publishing, venture capital and academia. She is based in the United States and has international experience working with partners in Europe, the UK, China and India.

Currently, Dr. Massey serves as President & CEO of J.D. Massey Associates, Inc. (JDMA), a communications consulting firm that advises clients on managing global brand reputation with an emphasis on communicating externally and internally with Millennial and Gen Z employees, consumers and investors. She is a sought-after corporate speaker and thought leader on the challenges and solutions to dealing with five generations in the workplace. She is also the author of the book, *Culture Shock: Surviving Five Generations in One Workplace.*

Prior to JDMA, Dr. Massey ran numerous communications departments reporting into presidents and CEOs. She was Head of Communications at Condé

Nast Entertainment; Senior Vice President, Corporate Communications at Lionsgate; Senior Vice President of Corporate Communications and Publicity at the Hub Network, a joint venture between Discovery and Hasbro; Senior Vice President, Communications, West Coast at CBS; Senior Vice President, Media Relations at UPN; and Vice President, PR, Marketing and New Business Development at the independent production company LMNO Productions. Dr. Massey began her career at the international PR firm Fleishman Hillard and then quickly transitioned to the media industry, working in-house as a senior publicist for the CBS Television Network.

In addition, Dr. Massey is an adjunct professor at Columbia University, where she teaches a graduate-level course in corporate communications and brand reputation management in the School of International and Public Affairs (SIPA).

Dr. Massey serves on corporate, startup and nonprofit boards and is a member of the National Association of Corporate Directors. Currently, she is on the Advisory Board of 8B Education Investments, a for-profit business providing innovative student-financing products for African students studying abroad at world-class universities. She is also on the Advisory Board of The Resolution Project, a nonprofit organization providing seed funding, mentorship and access to global advisory resources for undergraduate students who are developing entrepreneurial ventures that promote social good. In addition, Dr. Massey is an active fundraiser for The Chapin School and sits on both the development and planned giving committees. Formerly, she served on the Board of Directors of The Resolution Project as a member of the Audit committee, the University of Southern California New York Alumni Club as a member of the Executive Board, and Colors LGBTQ Youth Counseling Services.

Dr. Massey is also an angel investor. She previously served as a Managing Director at Golden Seeds, an early-stage female-led investment firm with more than $125 million in total investments in over 170 female run businesses. Dr. Massey advises entrepreneurs on investor decks, go-to market messaging and developing workplace culture. She is a member of the Angel Capital Association.

Dr. Massey's diverse professional background includes several years of higher education. She has a Graduate Certificate in Corporate Finance from Harvard, as well as an MBA from the University of Southern California, and two graduate degrees in psychology—a Master of Arts in Clinical Psychology from Antioch University Los Angeles, and a Doctorate in Transpersonal Psychology from Sofia University (formerly the Institute of Transpersonal Psychology). While receiving her psychology degrees, Dr. Massey served as a therapist in a community clinic and then as a personal coach working with individual clients and holding public workshops to help people recognize conditioned thinking and achieve higher levels of personal and professional success. Dr. Massey is a member of the American Psychological Association.

Dr. Massey was born and raised in New York City. She lived briefly in Paris studying French, and spent many years in Los Angeles, having originally moved there to attend USC as an undergraduate student, where she obtained a B.A. in journalism with an emphasis in public relations and a minor in philosophy with an emphasis in ethics.

ENDNOTES

[1] *Good Morning America*, Television newscast, Michael Strahan, Robin Roberts, George Stephanopoulos, ABC Television Network, March 19, 2020. https://twitter.com/GMA/status/124060431416443289 6?ref_src=twsrc%5Etfw%7Ctwcamp%5Etweetembed%7 Ctwterm%5E1240604314164432896&ref_url=https%3A% 2F%2Fwww.newsweek.com%2Fkylie-jenner-1493259 (retrieved April 12, 2020)

[2] *Good Morning America*, Television newscast, Michael Strahan, Robin Roberts, George Stephanopoulos, ABC Television Network, March 19, 2020. https://twitter.com/GMA/status/124060431416443289 6?ref_src=twsrc%5Etfw%7Ctwcamp%5Etweetembed%7 Ctwterm%5E1240604314164432896&ref_url=https%3A% 2F%2Fwww.newsweek.com%2Fkylie-jenner-1493259 (retrieved April 12, 2020)

[3] Washington Post Staff. "Mapping the Spread of the Coronavirus in the U.S. and Worldwide." *The Washington Post*, actively updated. https://www.washingtonpost.com/graphics/2020/wor ld/mapping-spread-new-coronavirus/ (retrieved March 21, 2020 at 12:50 PM Eastern Time)

[4] Wikipedia. "2020 Coronavirus Pandemic in the United States." Wikipedia, actively updated. https://en.wikipedia.org/wiki/2020_coronavirus_pand emic_in_the_United_States#Timeline (retrieved March 21, 2020 at 12:45 PM Eastern Time)

[5] Website page. "Coronavirus Disease 2019 (COVID-19): Cases in the U.S." Centers for Disease Control and Prevention, actively updated. https://www.cdc.gov/coronavirus/2019-ncov/cases-updates/cases-in-us.html (retrieved April 1, 2020)

[6] Website page. "2020 Coronavirus Pandemic in the United States." Wikipedia, actively updated. https://en.wikipedia.org/wiki/2020_coronavirus_pandemic_in_the_United_States (retrieved April 1, 2020)

[7] Winck, Ben. "Dow Plunges More than 2,000 Points, Biggest Decline Since 2008, as Coronavirus Fuels Market Turmoil." *Business Insider*, March 9, 2020. https://markets.businessinsider.com/news/stocks/stock-market-news-today-indexes-plunge-oil-market-coronavirus-selloff-2020-3-1028978137?op=1 (retrieved April 6, 2020)

[8] Website post. "Outbreak: 10 of the Worst Pandemics in History." MPH Online, actively updated. https://www.mphonline.org/worst-pandemics-in-history/ (retrieved March 21, 2020 at 2:30 PM Eastern Time)

[9] Dimock, Michael. "Defining Generations: Where Millennials End and Generation Z Begins." Pew Research Center, January 17, 2019. https://www.pewresearch.org/fact-tank/2019/01/17/where-millennials-end-and-generation-z-begins/ (retrieved March 29, 2020)

[10] Slater, Georgia. "Surgeon General Asks Kylie Jenner, Other Influencers to Speak Out About Seriousness of Coronavirus." *People Magazine*, March 19, 2020. https://people.com/style/surgeon-general-asks-kylie-jenner-influencers-speak-out-coronavirus/ (retrieved March 21, 2020)

[11] Guglielmi, Jodi. "Kylie Jenner Agrees with the Surgeon General's Coronavirus Warning: 'Please Stay Inside.'" *People Magazine*, March 20, 2020. https://people.com/tv/kylie-jenner-urges-followers-stay-inside-amid-the-coronavirus/ (retrieved March 21, 2020)

[12] Belfiore, Emily. "Kevin Bacon Encourages Social Distancing with Sweet '6 Degrees' Campaign." NBC New York, March 18, 2020. https://www.nbcnewyork.com/entertainment/entertainment-news/kevin-bacon-encourages-social-distancing-with-sweet-6-degrees-campaign/2333310/ (retrieved March 21, 2020)

[13] Hale, James. "World Health Organization Launches Daily Livestreamed Concert Series with Coldplay, John Legend, More." *Tubefilter*, March 17, 2020. https://www.tubefilter.com/2020/03/17/who-global-citizen-together-at-home-john-legend-instagram/ (retrieved March 21, 2020)

[14] Macaray, David. "The 2007-08 Writers Strike." *Huffington Post*, September 4, 2013. https://www.huffpost.com/entry/the-200708-writers-strike_b_3840681 (retrieved April 14, 2020)

[15] Website page. "Workplace Injuries." National Safety Council. https://www.nsc.org/work-safety/tools-resources/infographics/workplace-injuries (retrieved March 22, 2020)

[16] Website page. "Average Number of Own Children Under 18 in Families with Children in the United States from 1960 to 2019." Statista, actively updated. https://www.statista.com/statistics/718084/average-number-of-own-children-per-family/ (retrieved April 23, 2020)

[17] *Merriam-Webster*, s.v. "Perfect, adjective." https://www.merriam-webster.com/dictionary/perfect (retrieved March 26, 2020)

[18] *The Prison Within*. Dir. Katherin Hervey. Prod. Katherin Hervey and Erin Kenway. Gravitas Ventures, 2020. Film https://theprisonwithin.org

[19] *Merriam-Webster*, s.v. "Crisis, noun." https://www.merriam-webster.com/dictionary/crisis (retrieved March 21, 2020)

[20] Johnson, Spencer. *Who Moved My Cheese?* (New York: G.P. Putnam's Sons, 1998)

[21] *Oxford Reference*, s.v. "Unconscious Bias." https://www.oxfordreference.com/view/10.1093/oi/authority.20110803110609736 (retrieved March 22, 2020)

[22] *The Wizard of Oz*. Dir. Victor Fleming. Prod. Mervyn LeRoy. Metro-Goldwyn-Mayer (MGM), 1939. Film

[23] Rock, David. "SCARF: A Brain-Based Model for Collaborating with and Influencing Others." *NeuroLeadership Journal*, Issue One, 2008. http://web.archive.org/web/20100705024057/http://www.your-brain-at-work.com/files/NLJ_SCARFUS.pdf (retrieved March 24, 2020)

[24] Website page. "5 Stages of Grief." Elisabeth Kübler-Ross Foundation, no date. https://www.ekrfoundation.org/5-stages-of-grief/5-stages-grief/ (retrieved March 31, 2020)

[25] Tiffany, Kaitlyn. "America Is Thirsty for Anthony Fauci: What Is It About a Crisis That Can Turn Even a 79-Year-Old Immunologist into a Heartthrob?" *The Atlantic*, April 7, 2020. https://www.theatlantic.com/technology/archive/2020/04/anthony-fauci-coronavirus-crush/609544/ (retrieved April 12, 2020)

[26] Smith, Ben. "Andrew Cuomo Is the Control Freak We Need Right Now." *The New York Times*, March 16, 2020. https://www.nytimes.com/2020/03/16/business/media/cuomo-new-york-coronavirus.html (retrieved March 22, 2020)

[27] Fishbein, Rebecca. "Help, I Think I'm in Love with Andrew Cuomo???" *Jezebel*, March 19, 2020. https://jezebel.com/help-i-think-im-in-love-with-andrew-cuomo-1842396411 (retrieved March 22, 2020)

[28] Cuomo, Andrew. "Governor Cuomo Announces Distribution of Health Care Supplies to New York City Hospitals." NYGovCuomo YouTube Channel, March 24, 2020. https://www.youtube.com/watch?v=WoeIoSYSk50 (retrieved March 26, 2020)

[29] Cuomo, Andrew. "Governor Cuomo Announces Distribution of Health Care Supplies to New York City Hospitals." NYGovCuomo YouTube Channel, March 24, 2020. https://www.youtube.com/watch?v=WoeIoSYSk50 (retrieved March 26, 2020)

[30] Cuomo, Andrew. "Governor Cuomo Announces State Is Scouting New Sites for Temporary Hospitals Downstate." NYGovCuomo YouTube Channel, March 26, 2020. https://www.youtube.com/watch?v=VhVLFDak-w0 (retrieved March 26, 2020)

[31] *Business Dictionary*, s.v. "Crisis Communications." http://www.businessdictionary.com/definition/crisis-communication.html (retrieved March 27, 2020)

[32] Rovell, Darren. "Famed 'Be Like Mike' Gatorade Ad Debuted 25 Years Ago." ESPN.com, August 8, 2016. https://www.espn.com/nba/story/_/id/17246999/michael-jordan-famous-mike-gatorade-commercial-debuted-25-years-ago-monday (retrieved March 27, 2020)

[33] Dimock, Michael. "Defining Generations: Where Millennials End and Generation Z Begins." Pew Research Center, January 17, 2019. https://www.pewresearch.org/fact-tank/2019/01/17/where-millennials-end-and-generation-z-begins/ (retrieved March 29, 2020)

[34] Dimock, Michael. "Defining Generations: Where Millennials End and Generation Z Begins." Pew Research Center, January 17, 2019. https://www.pewresearch.org/fact-tank/2019/01/17/where-millennials-end-and-generation-z-begins/ (retrieved March 29, 2020)

[35] Hatton, Georgia. "Micro Influencers vs Macro Influencers." *Social Media Today*, February 13, 2018. https://www.socialmediatoday.com/news/micro-influencers-vs-macro-influencers/516896/ (retrieved April 5, 2020)

[36] McCrann, Takako. "Essay: Shame, Honor and Duty." PBS, no date. http://www.pbs.org/mosthonorableson/shame.html (retrieved March 27, 2020)

[37] Maxwell, John and Jim Dornan. *How to Influence People.* (Nashville, TN: Thomas Nelson Inc., 2013)

[38] Governor Andrew Cuomo. "Gov. Cuomo Holds Coronavirus Press Briefing." Live: April 10, 2020. Facebook video. 54:38. https://www.facebook.com/GovernorAndrewCuomo/videos/522419438444841/ (retrieved April 10, 2020)

[39] Website page. "What Does 'You Catch More Flies with Honey than with Vinegar' Mean?" Using English, no date. https://www.usingenglish.com/reference/idioms/you+can+catch+more+flies+with+honey+than+with+vinegar.html (retrieved March 29, 2020)

[40] Paul, Richard and Linda Elder. *The Thinker's Guide to the Art of Socratic Questioning*. (Tomales, CA: Foundation for Critical Thinking, 2006) https://www.criticalthinking.org/TGS_files/SocraticQuestioning2006.pdf (retrieved March 30, 2020)

[41] Schlottman, Andrea. "Leo Tolstoy's Infamous Quote: 'No One Thinks of Changing Himself.'" Books on the Wall, no date. https://booksonthewall.com/blog/leo-tolstoy-quote/ (retrieved April 1, 2020)

[42] Amlen, Deb. "Wordplay: 'We Do Not See Things as They Are.'" *The New York Times*, August 4, 2017. https://www.nytimes.com/2017/08/04/crosswords/daily-puzzle-2017-08-05.html (retrieved April 1, 2020)

CPSIA information can be obtained
at www.ICGtesting.com
Printed in the USA
BVHW041053030520
579089BV00015B/3682